KNITTED GOLF CLUB
Susie Johns
COVERS

Search Press

KNITTED GOLF CLUB COVERS

Susie Johns

A WHOLE BAG FULL OF PROJECTS TO KNIT

CONTENTS

INTRODUCTION

AT ITS BEST, the game of golf is a blend of skill and creativity; an involving and challenging way to spend your time that is still relaxing and enjoyable – and the same is true of knitting! This book contains a huge range of club covers and useful accessories to knit. Some of the covers make an elegant statement; some provide an opportunity to display your team or club colours – or even match your golfing sweater – while others rely unashamedly on their novelty value.

On a practical level, covers will protect your clubs as you move round the course, which helps to avoid nicks and scratches during play. This is important because a scratched driver head is much more likely to slice the ball. However, it's not just about protection: covers stop the clubs from rattling around in the golf bag, and they also make it easy and quick to identify the club you want.

The patterns are easy, even for the inexperienced knitter, and they are a great way of using up yarn left over from other projects. Whether you choose to knit a set for yourself, or for a golfing friend or family member, these fun and rewarding projects will become a real talking point on the course.

BEFORE YOU TEE OFF

Golf rewards proper preparation, and this applies equally to knitting. Familiarity with the techniques will make a difference to your working process, and updating your knowledge and skills with needles and yarn will make knitting your golf club covers a lot easier and more enjoyable.

The following pages look at the tools, materials and techniques you will need to make the golf club covers in this book. If you are an experienced knitter, you may wish to skip straight to the patterns, but a little pre-knitting refresher is always useful.

The Devil's luck

Most golfers have had one of those dreadful rounds where nothing seems to go right. Making a devil's head might be just what you need to scare off bad luck – or pass it on to the other players! The pattern and instructions for this cover can be found on pages 68–71.

KNITTING BASICS

Due to their relatively small size, the projects in this book are quick to make – and easy too, using two needles. You don't need to be a knitting expert: rudimentary knowledge should be enough. You will need to know how to cast on and off, knit and purl, and, in a couple of instances, work short-row shaping.

Three of the projects – *Numbers*, *Argyle* and *Pirates* (see pages 24, 28 and 96 respectively) – involve slightly more complete colourwork techniques of intarsia and Fair Isle.

When working increases and decreases, various methods are used. Be aware that increasing by knitting into the front and back of a stitch (kfb) is different from increasing by knitting into the loop in front of a stitch (M1) and the two methods are not interchangeable, so follow the instructions in the pattern carefully.

You will also need to know how to sew pieces together and, as these covers are relatively small, you will need to do this neatly. Untidy stitching will be evident and might spoil the appearance of the finished item. Most of the covers are made up in the same way, with a single seam; instructions for doing this are given in the basic pattern (see page 18), with any additional instructions provided within the individual patterns.

Blocking

Before sewing up, you may want to block the knitted pieces. Blocking – which involves either dampening the pieces, pinning them out into the required shape, and leaving to dry, or lightly steaming, or pressing lightly with a damp cloth – will help to create a neat result. The method you use will depend on the fibre content of your chosen yarn, so check the yarn band for advice.

Details

Embroidery skills are an asset when it comes to adding details. The stitches used in this book are satin stitch, Swiss darning and chain stitch (see pages 14, 15 and 15 respectively).

Abbreviations

The abbreviations listed below are the most frequently used terms in the book.

beg: begin(ning)

dec: decrease

DK: double knitting

k: knit

k2tog: knit two stitches together

kfb: knit into the front and back of the stitch, to increase one stitch

LH: left-hand

M1: increase by knitting into the loop in front of the next stitch

p: purl

p2tog: purl two stitches together

psso: pass slipped stitch over

rem: remain(ing)

rep: repeat(ing)

RH: right-hand

RS: right side

skpo: slip one stitch, knit next stitch, pass slipped stitch over

sl1: slip one stitch on to the right-hand needle without knitting it

st(s): stitch(es)

st st: stocking (stockinette) stitch

tbl: through back loop

trs: transfer

WS: wrong side

yfwd: yarn forward

yo: yarn over

MATERIALS

Yarn

Double knitting yarn, known as DK, light worsted or 8-ply, is the most popular yarn weight – it is likely that you will already have some in your stash. It has been used throughout, the only exceptions being *Octopuses* on page 100, which uses aran (worsted/10-ply) weight yarn – though this could also be made using two strands of DK (light worsted/8-ply) instead, if you like.

For most of the projects, pure wool yarns or wool-rich blends have been used: this is because wool is naturally springy and elastic, allowing it to stretch and spring back into shape. It is also fairly waterproof. You may prefer to use yarns made from other fibres, however. The snowman family on page 72, *Snake Charmer* on page 80 and *Fuzzy* on page 60 were made using acrylic yarns, for example. Synthetic yarns tend to be more brightly coloured and are also cheaper.

Cotton yarns are another popular choice with many knitters, as these yarns are soft and comfortable to work with, and cotton knits are easy to care for. Cotton yarn is not as stretchy as wool, however, and can lose its shape. The *Stars & Stripes* covers on page 56 are made with cotton but could just as well be made using a wool yarn; the *Tweedy* set on page 40 are made from a cotton yarn and, to allow for its lack of elasticity, each cover is made slightly larger than the others in the book, and also features a row of eyelets threaded with elastic to help keep it in place.

Needles

The recommended needle size for standard double-knitting yarns is 4mm (UK 8; US 6). This is supposed to produce a standard tension of 22 stitches and 28 rows measured over 10cm (4in). Check the ball band of the yarn for this information. For the golf head covers, 3.25mm (UK 10; US 3) needles are used for the ribbed sections, which cover the shaft of the club; then the yarn is, in most cases, used double for the top part of the cover, which fits over the head. 4mm (UK 8; US 6) needles have been used to create a firm, thick fabric to cushion and protect the golf club.

Other materials

You will need a tapestry needle for sewing up, and scissors for snipping yarn ends.

TENSION

Knit up a tension square for the yarn you are using. For the projects in this book, you should aim for a tension of 20 stitches and 26 rows to 10cm (4in) with the yarn used double.

If your sample has fewer stitches to 10cm (4in), you should use a smaller needle; if it has more stitches, use a larger needle.

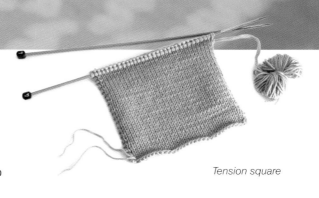

Tension square

POMPOMS

A number of the covers incorporate pompoms. For making pompoms you need nothing more sophisticated than some scrap card, though you may wish to treat yourself to a plastic pompom maker, which makes the task much quicker.

Finished pompom

Making pompoms

Pompoms are very popular with golfers and add a woolly flourish. You might have learned how to make pompoms with the time-honoured method of winding yarn around a pair of rings cut from scrap cardboard. However, once you have made a pompom using a plastic pompom maker, there will be no going back.

Either way, the method is more or less the same: wind the yarn round and round the rings until you have a fat bundle, then use sharp scissors to snip all round, through the strands, tie a length of yarn tightly around the middle, remove the rings (cardboard or plastic), then fluff up the pompom and trim to a neat rounded shape.

Scrap cardboard

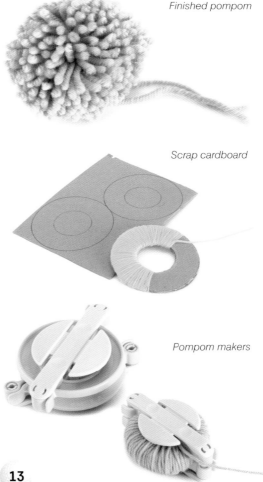

Pompom makers

EYES

Some of the character covers have knitted or embroidered eyes, while some have plastic eyes. You can use flat, sew-on googly eyes like those used for the *Eagle* and *Albatross* (see pages 52 and 64 respectively), or you can use safety eyes, which comprise a plastic eye with a short rod that you push through the knitted fabric and secure on the inside with a washer.

A selection of toy safety eyes and googly eyes.

To prevent the end of the rod from scratching the golf club, after fixing the eyes in place, cover the washer on the inside with a circle of felt and stitch it in place with a matching thread (see below). This will keep the rod from scratching the head of the club when in use.

The eye from the front.

A circle of felt stitched in place to protect the cover from the rod.

SATIN STITCH

Used to fill a small area such as the pupil of an eye, or a nose, this embroidery stitch simply comprises a series of straight, parallel stitches. Do not pull the yarn too tightly, as you may distort the knitted fabric.

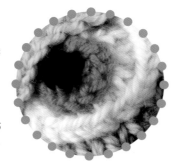

Satin stitch was used for the pupil of Nessie's eye. See pages 32–35 for the cover pattern.

CHAIN STITCH

This is a looped stitch, useful for creating thick lines. Thread a tapestry needle with yarn, bring it up through the knitted fabric at the beginning of the line; then back down at the same place; then up again a short way along the line, making sure the needle tip comes up through the loop of yarn.

Chain stitch makes for great detailing on the Tiger. *See pages 44–47 for the cover pattern.*

SWISS DARNING

This is a method of embroidering a stitch that looks like a knit stitch – and is sometimes called 'duplicate' stitch, for this reason. It is mostly used to work single motifs or small details in a contrast colour; it can also sometimes be used instead of the intarsia method.

Thread a tapestry needle with a length of yarn. Bring the point of the needle through from back to front at the base of the stitch to be covered and pull the yarn through, leaving the yarn end at the back of the work. Take the needle from right to left behind the two loops of the stitch above, pull the yarn through, then re-insert the needle into the same place from which it came out at the beginning. To work the next stitch, bring the needle through to the front at the base of the next stitch to be covered, and continue in this way until the line of stitches, or the motif, is complete.

Swiss darning is used to create the impression of vertical lines in the tartan plaid for the project on pages 36–39.

I-CORD

This produces a neat, rounded cord with a stocking stitch appearance. You need to use needles with a point at each end.

Simply cast on a small number of stitches and knit as usual – but do not turn the work. Instead, slide the stitches along to the other end of the double-pointed needle. Knit the first stitch, taking note of the fact that the working yarn is hanging from the stitch on the far left and you will have to pull it a bit tighter than you normally would when knitting a stitch.

Continue to knit the remaining stitches in the row then, once again, do not turn the work but slide the stitches back to the other end of the needle and repeat the process. Each time you start a new row, give the first stitch a little tug, to prevent a gap forming.

The tentacles of the octopus covers are made using i-cords. The project is on pages 100–103.

BASIC COVERS

Most of the patterns in the book use this simple pattern to form the basis of the cover, with various embellishments. Where this is the case, the instructions will make reference to the basic pattern.

Like many of the others, the basic cover can be made in one of three sizes: to fit a 5-wood, a 3-wood or a driver. Of course, there's no reason why you can't make a set of three in matching colours instead of the pastel mix shown here.

Measurements and sizes

The instructions given are for a cover to fit a 5-wood, with instructions for the larger 3-wood and driver covers given in brackets.

The basic cover measures 12 (13, 14.5)cm/4¾ (5¼, 5¾)in long, not including the ribbed section; and 20 (25, 30)cm/8 (10, 12)in circumference at the widest part.

YOU WILL NEED

- 50g DK (light worsted/8-ply) yarn in primrose (A), pale blue (B) and pale pink (C). Choose a double knitting yarn that knits to a standard DK (light worsted/8-ply) tension.
- Needles: 3.25mm (UK 10; US 3) and 4mm (UK 8; US 6)
- Tapestry needle

TENSION

20 sts and 26 rows to 10cm (4in), measured over stocking stitch using 4mm (UK 8; US 6) needles, with two strands of yarn.

KNITTING THE COVERS

Note that a single strand of yarn is used for the ribbed part of the cover, and two strands for the top part.

Using 3.25mm (UK 10; US 3) needles and yarn A (B, C), cast on 24 (30, 36) sts.

Row 1 (RS): *k1, p1; rep from * to end.

Next rows: Rep row 1 27 (31, 35) times more.

Change to 4mm (UK 8; US 6) needles and begin using the yarn held double.

Row 1 (RS): k to end.

Row 2 (WS): p to end.

Row 3: (k5, kfb) 4 (5, 6) times. 28 (35, 42) sts.

Row 4: p to end.

Row 5: (k6, kfb) 4 (5, 6) times. 32 (40, 48) sts.

Next rows: Beg with a WS row, work 13 (17, 21) rows in st st.

Shaping

Shape top as follows:

Row 1 (RS): (k6, k2tog) to end. 28 (35, 42) sts

Row 2 (and every WS row): p to end.

Row 3: (k5, k2tog) to end. 24 (30, 36) sts

Row 5: (k4, k2tog) to end. 20 (35, 30) sts

Row 7: (k3, k2tog) to end. 16 (20, 24) sts

Row 9: (k2, k2tog) to end. 12 (15, 18) sts

Row 11: (k1, k2tog) to end. 8 (10, 12) sts

Row 12: (p2tog) to end. 4 (5, 6) sts

Cut yarn, leaving a long tail, and thread tail through rem sts.

To make up

1 Pull up the tail of the yarn to gather stitches at the top of the cover.

2 Fold the cover in half with right sides together and stitch the side edges together with a back stitch seam (alternatively, stitch seam from right side using mattress stitch).

3 Turn right side out to finish.

STRIPED COVER SET

Designed as an eye-catching set of club covers, there will be no missing you on the course with these in your bag. Using small amounts of wool for each stripe, this project offers a great opportunity to sort out your stash and combine leftover scraps from other projects to make colourful covers that will really stand out on the golf course.

With that said, the rainbow examples here are just one possibility; you can buy specific contrasting or complementary colours if you want to create a particular pattern – black and yellow would make a fun bee-themed set, for example – or you might want to make a set in your club colours.

Measurements and sizes

As for the basic cover on page 16. The instructions given are for a cover to fit a 5-wood, with instructions for the larger 3-wood and driver covers given in brackets.

YOU WILL NEED

- Approximately 100g total DK (light worsted/8-ply) yarn. Choose a yarn that knits to a standard DK (light worsted/8-ply) tension.
- Needles: 3.25mm (UK 10; US 3) and 4mm (UK 8; US 6)
- Tapestry needle

TENSION

20 sts and 26 rows to 10cm (4in), measured over stocking stitch using 4mm (UK 8; US 6) needles, with two strands of yarn.

22

KNITTING THE COVERS

First rows: With 3.25mm (UK 10; US 3) needles and your chosen yarn, cast on 24 (30, 36) sts and follow the basic pattern on page 18 for the ribbed section.

Next rows: Change to 4mm (UK 8; US 6) needles and another yarn colour (using the yarn held double) and follow the pattern instructions to complete the cover, changing colours after every fourth row.

To make up

Follow the making-up instructions for the basic cover on page 18. Use yarn scraps to make pompoms (see page 13) and stitch or tie one securely to the top of each cover.

As with the other covers in the book, the ribbed section can be rolled down to cover more of the shaft, as shown here, or rolled up as in the picture on the previous pages, which will make the club covers look like a matching set of bobble hats.

NUMBERED COVER SET

With clearly labelled numbers, it is easier and quicker to identify the club you want. This eye-catching trio is designed for the driver, and 3- and 5-woods. Knit them in your club colours, or simply choose harmonious shades of yarn.

Measurements and sizes

As for the basic cover on page 16. The instructions given are for a cover to fit a 5-wood, with instructions for the larger 3-wood and driver covers given in brackets.

YOU WILL NEED

- 50g of DK (light worsted/8-ply) yarn in red (A), raspberry (B), burnt orange (C), ivory (D) and navy blue (E). Choose a yarn that knits to a standard DK (light worsted/8-ply) tension.
- Needles: 3.25mm (UK 10; US 3) and 4mm (UK 8; US 6)
- Tapestry needle

TENSION

20 sts and 26 rows to 10cm (4in), measured over stocking stitch using 4mm (UK 8; US 6) needles, with two strands of yarn.

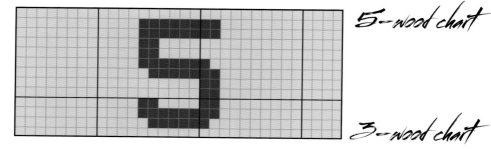

5-wood chart

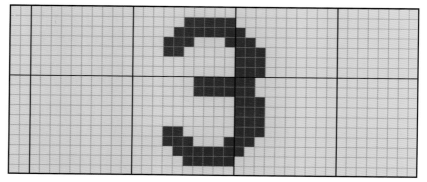

3-wood chart

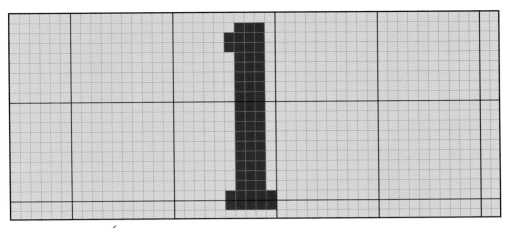

Driver chart

KNITTING THE COVERS

Be aware that one strand of yarn is used for the ribbed part of the cover, and two strands of yarn for the Head. The numbers are worked using the intarsia method, following the charts shown below. On WS rows, read the charts from left to right; on RS rows, read the charts from right to left. If you prefer, you can add the numbers afterwards, using Swiss darning (see page 15).

First rows: Using 3.25mm (UK 10; US 3) needles and yarn A (B, C), cast on 24 (30, 36) sts. Follow the basic pattern on page 18 for the ribbed section and first 5 rows of the top part, changing to 4mm (UK 8; US 6) needles and yarn held double as indicated.

Next row (WS): Fasten off yarn A (B, C), change to yarn D, and work row 1 of chart to end, being aware that row 1 of the chart is a WS row, worked in purl, and should be read from left to right.

Next rows: Continue working from chart using yarns D and E and the intarsia method until chart has been completed once.

Fasten off yarn D, rejoin A (B, C) and complete the cover by following the basic pattern to shape the top.

To make up

Follow the making-up instructions for the basic cover on page 18.

ARGYLE

ARGYLE COVER SET

The distinctive Argyle diamond pattern is a classic. Popular on the golf course for nearly a hundred years, it has many permutations and endless colour combinations. The Duke of Windsor made it fashionable in the 1920s and even today many golfers favour Argyle patterns on jumpers and socks. So why not make a set of Argyle covers in the colours of your choice?

Measurements and sizes

As for the basic cover on page 16. The instructions given are for a cover to fit a 5-wood, with instructions for the larger 3-wood and driver covers given in brackets.

YOU WILL NEED

- 50g of DK (light worsted/8-ply) yarn in mustard (A), navy blue (B), blue (C), ivory (D) and beige (E). Choose a double knitting yarn that knits to a standard DK (light worsted/8-ply) tension.
- Needles: 3.25mm (UK 10; US 3) and 4mm (UK 8; US 6)
- Tapestry needle

TENSION

20 sts and 26 rows to 10cm (4in), measured over stocking stitch using 4mm (UK 8; US 6) needles, with two strands of yarn.

KNITTING THE COVERS

Fair Isle knitting uses no more than two colours of yarn in any one row. Each of the charts (opposite) begins with a purl row: purl rows are read from left to right and knit rows from right to left. The chart indicates which colour to use for each stitch. Carry the colour not in use loosely across the back of the work.

First rows: Using 3.25mm (UK 10; US 3) needles and yarn A (B, C), cast on 24 (30, 36) sts and follow basic pattern (see page 18) for ribbed section and first 5 rows of the top part, changing to 4mm (UK 8; US 6) needles and yarn held double as indicated.

Next row (WS): Work row 1 of chart to end, introducing yarn D (A, E) where indicated, and using the Fair Isle method to create the Argyle design.

Next rows: Continue working from the appropriate chart until chart has been completed once.

Fasten off yarn D (A, E), continue with yarn A (B, C) only and complete the cover by following the basic pattern to shape top.

To make up

Follow the making-up instructions for the basic cover on page 18. Using leftover yarn, make three pompoms in various sizes, and stitch or tie firmly to the top of each of the covers.

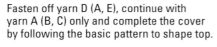

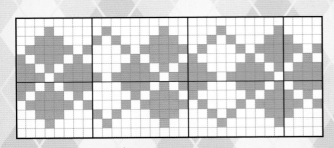

5-wood chart

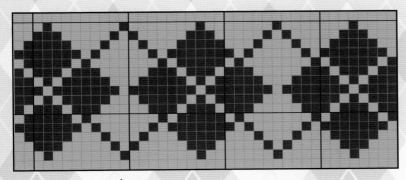

3-wood chart

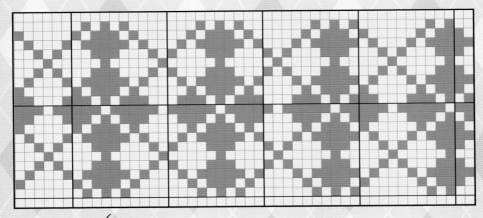

Driver chart

NESSIE

NESSIE COVER

There is only one monster in Loch Ness – as far as we know –
and here he is in his knitted splendour, ready to guard your largest
golf club. Use your family tartan, if you have one, for his fabric
tam-o'-shanter hat.

Measurements and sizes

To fit a driver. This cover measures 14.5cm (5¾in) long (not
including the hat); 30cm (12in) circumference at widest part.

YOU WILL NEED

- 100g of DK (light worsted/8-ply) yarn in light green (A), 50g in
  sage green (B) and ivory (C), and small amounts of turquoise
  (D) and black (E). Choose a double knitting yarn that knits to a
  standard DK (light worsted/8-ply) tension.
- Needles: 3.25mm (UK 10; US 3) and 4mm (UK 8; US 6)
- Tapestry needle
- Toy stuffing
- Tartan fabric, about 20cm (8in) square
- Sewing thread to match fabric

TENSION

20 sts and 26 rows to 10cm (4in), measured over stocking stitch
using 4mm (UK 8; US 6) needles, with two strands of yarn.

KNITTING THE COVER

Be aware that one strand of yarn is used for the ribbed part of the cover, and two strands of yarn for the head.

First rows: Using 3.25mm (UK 10; US 3) needles and yarn A, cast on 36 sts and follow the basic pattern (see page 18) in the largest size, changing to 4mm (UK 8; US 6) needles and yarn held double as indicated.

Muzzle

Using 3.25mm (UK 10; US 3) needles and a single strand of yarn B, cast on 6 sts.

Row 1 and every WS row: p to end.

Row 2 (RS): kfb to end (12 sts).

Row 4: kfb to end (24 sts).

Row 6: (k3, kfb) to end (30 sts).

Row 8: (k4, kfb) to end (36 sts).

Row 10: (k5, kfb) to end (42 sts).

Row 12: (k6, kfb) to end (48 sts).

Row 14: (k7, kfb) to end (54 sts).

Next rows: Beg with a p row, work 5 rows in st st.
Cast off.

Eyeball (make 2)

Using 3.25mm (UK 10; US 3) needles and a single strand of yarn C, cast on 10 sts.

Row 1: kfb to end (20 sts).

Row 2: p to end.
Cast off.

Iris (make 2)

Using 3.25mm (UK 10; US 3) needles and a single strand of yarn D, cast on 6 sts.

Row 1: kfb to end (12 sts).

Row 2: k to end.
Cut yarn and thread tail through all sts.

Eyelid (make 2)

Using 3.25mm (UK 10; US 3) needles and a single strand of A, cast on 3 sts

Row 1: kfb to end (6 sts).

Row 2: p to end.

Row 3: k1, kfb, k2, kfb, k1 (8 sts).

Row 4: p to end.

Row 5: k1, kfb, k4, kfb, k1 (10 sts).

Row 6: p to end.
Cast off.

The tam-o'-shanter

1 Cut a circle, 18cm (7in) in diameter, from tartan fabric. Using matching sewing thread, sew a running stitch around the circumference.

2 Pull up the thread to gather into a beret shape, adding a little stuffing if you wish, and stitch to the top of the head.

3 Make a pompom using yarn C and stitch it to the centre of the tam-o'-shanter, taking the yarn right through and fastening off securely on the inside of the head.

Detail of the tam-o'-shanter.

To make up

1 Follow the making-up instructions for the basic cover on page 18.

2 For the Muzzle, stitch the side seam, then pin the cast-off edge in place on the front of the head, with the lower edge touching the top of the ribbed section. Stitch in place, adding stuffing as you go.

3 Stitch the seams on the Eyeballs and Irises, then stitch them in place above the Muzzle.

4 Embroider the centre of the eyes in satin stitch using black yarn, then stitch an Eyelid over the top part of each eye.

5 Embroider a curved line for the mouth, in chain stitch, and two small nostrils in satin stitch.

Detail of Nessie's eyes.

TARTAN COVER SET

It is generally accepted that golf has its origins in Scotland, perhaps when, in the ancient mists of time, a lonely shepherd might have hit a stone with the end of his crook? The first documented evidence of the word 'golf' is when King James II banned 'ye golf' in 1457, in an attempt to encourage archery practice instead. So, to celebrate its origins, here is a set of covers inspired by Scottish tartans.

Measurements and sizes

As for the basic cover on page 16. The instructions given are for a cover to fit a 5-wood, with instructions for the larger 3-wood and driver covers given in brackets.

Detail of the pompoms.

YOU WILL NEED

- 50g of DK (light worsted/8-ply) yarn in bottle green (A), red (B), cream (C) and white (D). Choose a double knitting yarn that knits to a standard DK (light worsted/8-ply) tension.
- Needles: 3.25mm (UK 10; US 3) and 4mm (UK 8; US 6)
- Tapestry needle

TENSION

20 sts and 26 rows to 10cm (4in), measured over stocking stitch using 4mm (UK 8; US 6) needles, with two strands of yarn.

KNITTING THE COVERS

The horizontal stripes are knitted in the central section of the head cover, changing colours as indicated in the pattern instructions below. The vertical lines that transform the stripes into a tartan pattern are worked at the making-up stage, using the Swiss darning technique on page 15.

First rows: Using 3.25mm (UK 10; US 3) needles and yarn A (B, C), cast on 24 (30, 36) sts and follow the pattern for the basic cover for the ribbed section and first 4 rows of the top part, changing to 4mm (UK 8; US 6) needles and yarn held double as indicated.

Next rows: Continue to follow the basic pattern on page 18, changing colours as follows and carrying yarn not in use loosely up the side of the work:

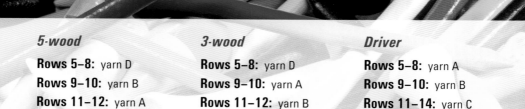

5-wood
Rows 5–8: yarn D
Rows 9–10: yarn B
Rows 11–12: yarn A
Rows 13–14: yarn B
Rows 15–18: yarn D

3-wood
Rows 5–8: yarn D
Rows 9–10: yarn A
Rows 11–12: yarn B
Rows 13–14: yarn D
Rows 15–16: yarn B
Rows 17–18: yarn A
Rows 19–22: yarn D

Driver
Rows 5–8: yarn A
Rows 9–10: yarn B
Rows 11–14: yarn C
Rows 15–16: yarn A
Rows 17–20: yarn C
Rows 21–22: yarn B
Rows 23–26: yarn A

All sizes
Fasten off yarn D (D, A), rejoin A (B, C), and complete the cover by following the basic pattern on page 18 to shape top.

To make up

1 Using one strand of yarn embroider vertical lines of Swiss darning over the striped section of each cover, referring to the picture of the finished covers.

2 Then follow the making-up instructions given in the basic pattern.

3 Using leftover yarn, make three pompoms in various sizes, and stitch or tie firmly to the top of each of the covers.

Bonnie Scotland

Making a matching set of club covers is a great way to personalise your bag. This tartan set works beautifully on its own, but matching it with Nessie (see pages 32–35) makes a great themed set.

TWEED COVER SET

The understated classic appearance of tweed looks just right on the golf course, especially when you add some fluffy pompoms.

Made from cotton yarn, which has less stretch than wool, this trio of head covers is made slightly larger, and with elastic to help them stay on.

Measurements and sizes

The instructions given are for a cover to fit a 5-wood, with instructions for the larger 3-wood and driver covers given in brackets.

Length (not including pompom): 19 (20, 21)cm/7½ (8, 8¼)in.
Circumference: 24 (26, 32)cm/9½ (10¼, 12½)in

YOU WILL NEED

- 50g of DK (light worsted/8-ply) yarn in brown (A), aqua (B) and grey (D), and 100g in beige (C). Choose a cotton double knitting yarn that knits to a standard DK (light worsted/8-ply) tension
- Needles: 3.25mm (UK 10; US 3) and 4.5mm (UK 7; US 7)
- Tapestry needle
- Sewing needle
- 50cm (20in) of 12mm (¾in) wide elastic
- Sewing thread to match elastic

TENSION

20 sts and 26 rows to 10cm (4in), measured over stocking stitch using 4.5mm (UK 7; US 7) needles, with two strands of yarn.

KNITTING THE COVERS

Be aware that one strand of yarn is used for the ribbed part of the cover, and two strands of yarn for the head.

Using 3.25mm (UK 10; US 3) needles and yarn A (B, C), cast on 32 (36, 40) sts.

Row 1 (RS): (k1, p1) to end.

Next rows: Repeat row 1 twenty-three times more.

Row 25 (eyelet row): k1, (yo, k2tog) to last st, p1.

Row 26: (k1, p1) to end.

Change to 4.5mm (UK 7; US 7) needles and use yarn held double.

Row 27: k to end.

Row 28: p to end.

Row 29: [k7 (8, 9), kfb] twice, [kfb, k7 (8, 9)] twice (36 (40, 44) sts).

Next rows: Beg with a p row, work 5 (5, 7) rows in st st.

Next row: [k8 (9, 10), kfb] twice, [kfb, k8 (9, 10)] twice (40 (44, 48) sts).

Next rows: Beg with a p row, work 3 (5, 5) rows in st st.

Next row: [k9 (10, 11), kfb] twice, [kfb, k9 (10, 11)] twice (44 (48, 52) sts).

Next rows: Beg with a p row, work 5 (5, 7) rows in st st.

Shaping the tops

5-wood only

Row 1 (RS): (k9, k2tog) twice, (k2tog, k9) twice (40 sts).

Row 2 (WS): (p3, p2tog) four times, (p2tog, p3) four times (32 sts).

Row 3: (k2, k2tog) four times, (k2tog, k2) four times (24 sts).

Row 4: (p1, p2tog) four times, (p2tog, p1) four times (16 sts).

Row 5: (k2tog) eight times (8 sts).

Row 6: (p2tog) four times (4 sts).

Cut yarn, leaving a long tail, and thread tail through rem sts.

3-wood only

Row 1 (RS): (k4, k2tog) four times, (k2tog, k4) four times (40 sts).

Row 2 (WS): (p3, p2tog) four times, (p2tog, p3) four times (32 sts).

Row 3: (k2, k2tog) four times, (k2tog, k2) four times (24 sts).

Row 4: (p1, p2tog) four times, (p2tog, p1) four times (16 sts).

Row 5: (k2tog) eight times (8 sts).

Row 6: (p2tog) four times (4 sts).

Cut yarn, leaving a long tail, and thread tail through rem sts.

Detail of the pompom.

Detail of the elastic.

Driver only

Row 1 (RS): (k11, k2tog) twice, (k2tog, k11) twice (48 sts).

Row 2 (WS): (p4, p2tog) four times, (p2tog, p4) four times (40 sts).

Row 3: (k3, k2tog) four times, (k2tog, k3) four times (32 sts).

Row 4: (p2, p2tog) four times, (p2tog, p2) four times (24 sts).

Row 5: (k1, k2tog) four times, (k2tog, k1) four times (16 sts).

Row 6: (p2tog) eight times (8 sts).

Row 7: (k2tog) four times (4 sts).

Cut yarn, leaving a long tail, and thread tail through rem sts.

To make up

1 Pull up tail of yarn to gather stitches at top of cover. Fold cover in half with right sides together and stitch side edges together with a backstitch seam (alternatively, stitch seam from right side using mattress stitch). Turn right side out.

2 Cut a 12 (14, 16)cm (4¾ (5½, 6¼) in) length of elastic and thread through eyelets. Stitch the ends together.

3 Make large pompoms using yarn D, and stitch or tie firmly in place.

TIGER COVER

Adapted from the pattern for the largest of the three head covers in the basic pattern on page 18, this cover is longer, so it is a good choice for an oversized driver. The padding in the muzzle adds extra layers of protection for your club. Perhaps more importantly, it helps bulk out the front of the cover to make sure it looks great on the course!

I can't guarantee that this tiger cover will make you play like his namesake, but the bold styling and colour will certainly raise a smile.

Measurements and sizes

To fit a driver or oversized driver. This cover measures 28cm (11in) long; 30cm (12in) in circumference at widest part.

YOU WILL NEED

- 50g of DK (light worsted/8-ply) yarn in black (A) and ivory (C), and 100g in orange (B). Choose a double knitting yarn that knits to a standard DK (light worsted/ 8-ply) tension.
- Needles: 3.25mm (UK 10; US 3) and 4mm (UK 8; US 6)
- Tapestry needle
- Toy stuffing
- Two 24mm (1in) amber-coloured toy safety eyes

TENSION

20 sts and 26 rows to 10cm (4in), measured over stocking stitch using 4mm (UK 8; US 6) needles, with two strands of yarn.

KNITTING THE COVER

Using 3.25mm (UK 10; US 3) needles and yarn A, cast on 36 sts. Following the basic pattern for the largest size, work the ribbed section, changing to yarn B after four rows, then alternating colours every four rows to create stripes. Fasten off yarn A, change to 4mm (UK 8; US 6) needles and use yarn B held double, and continue following the pattern to the end, working an additional 15 rows after the 21 rows in the centre section to create a longer cover.

Muzzle

Using 4mm (UK 8; US 6) needles and two strands of yarn C, cast on 6 sts.

Row 1 and every WS row: p to end.

Row 2: kfb to end (12 sts).

Row 4: (kfb to end (24 sts).

Row 6: (k3, kfb) to end (30 sts).

Row 8: (k4, kfb) to end (36 sts).

Row 10: (k5, kfb) to end (42 sts).

Row 12: (k6, kfb) to end (48 sts).

Row 14: (k7, kfb) to end (54 sts).

Next rows: Beg with a p row, work 5 rows in st st. Cast off.

Nose Strip

Using 3.25mm (UK 10; US 3) needles and a single strand of yarn B, cast on 2 sts.

Row 1 (WS): p to end.

Row 2 (RS): k1, M1, k1 (3 sts).

Row 3: p to end.

Row 4: (k1, M1) twice, k1 (5 sts).

Row 5: p to end.

Row 6: k1, M1, k to last st, M1, k1 (2 sts inc).

Next rows: Rep rows 5 and 6 three times more (13 sts).

Next rows: Beg with a p row, work 15 rows in st st. Cast off.

Ear (make 2)

Using 3.25mm (UK 10; US 3) needles and a single strand of yarn B, cast on 18 sts.

Row 1: p to end.

Row 2: k1, skpo, k5, M1, k2, M1, k5, k2tog, k1.

Row 3: p to end.

Next rows: Rep rows 2 and 3 five times more.

Row 14: k1, skpo, k to last 3 sts, k2tog, k1 (2 sts dec).

Row 15: p to end

Next rows: Rep rows 14 and 15 three times more (10 sts).

Fasten off yarn B and join in yarn A.

Row 22: k1, skpo, k to last 3 sts, k2tog, k1 (2 sts dec).

Row 23: p to end.

Next rows: Rep rows 22 and 23 once more (6 sts).

Row 26: k1, skpo, k2tog, k1 (4 sts).

Row 27: p to end.

Row 28: skpo, k2tog (2 sts).

Cut yarn and thread tail through rem sts.

Ear Lining (make 2)

Using 3.25mm (UK 10; US 3) needles and a single strand of yarn C, cast on 16 sts.

Beg with a p row, work 13 rows in st st.

Row 14: k2tog, k to last 2 sts, k2tog (2 sts dec).

Row 15: p to end.

Next rows: Rep rows 14 and 15 until 4 sts rem.

Cast off.

To make up

1 Pull up tail of yarn to gather stitches at top of cover. Fold cover in half with right sides together and stitch side edges together with a backstitch seam (alternatively, stitch seam from right side using mattress stitch). Turn right side out.

2 Stitch an Ear Lining to each Ear and stitch Ears to Head.

3 For the Muzzle, stitch the side seam, then pin the cast-off edge in place on the front of the head, with the lower edge two rows above the top of the ribbed section and the seam on the underside. Stitch in place, adding stuffing as you go.

4 Stitch the Nose Strip in place on the top part of the Muzzle. Insert the toy safety eyes and fix in place, then thread the tapestry needle with a length of black yarn and, in chain stitch, embroider around eyes, embroider a mouth, and create a few stripes on the face, the Muzzle and the backs of the Ears.

Detail of the back seam and ear detailing.

BIRDIE

BIRDIE COVER

'Birdie', the golfing term for a score of one stroke under par, is thought to have originated in the United States in the early twentieth century, when the slang term 'bird' meant excellent. This birdie cover might just bring its owner some luck on the fairway.

Measurements and sizes

To fit a driver. This cover measures 14.5cm (50¾in) long; 30cm (12in) circumference at widest part.

YOU WILL NEED

- 100g of DK (light worsted/8-ply) yarn in brown (A), and small amount of yellow (B). Choose a double knitting yarn that knits to a standard DK (light worsted/8-ply) tension.
- Needles: 3.25mm (UK 10; US 3) and 4mm (UK 8; US 6)
- Tapestry needle
- Two 15mm (½in) blue toy safety eyes
- Scrap of blue felt

TENSION

20 sts and 26 rows to 10cm (4in), measured over stocking stitch using 4mm (UK 8; US 6) needles, with two strands of yarn.

KNITTING THE COVER

Using 3.25mm (UK 10; US 3) needles and yarn A, cast on 36 sts and follow the basic pattern in the largest size, changing to 4mm (UK 8; US 6) needles and yarn held double as indicated.

Wing (make 2)

Using 3.25mm (UK 10; US 3) needles and a single strand of yarn A, cast on 3 sts.

Row 1: kfb, k to last st, kfb (2 sts inc).

Next rows: Rep row 1 six times more (17 sts).

Row 8: kfb, k to end (1 st inc).

Next rows: Rep row 8 nine times more (27 sts).

Next rows: Knit 8 rows.

Row 26: k10, skpo, k3, k2tog, k to end (25 sts).

Row 27 and every WS row: k to end.

Row 28: k9, skpo, k3, k2tog, k to end (23 sts).

Row 30: k8, skpo, k3, k2tog, k to end (21 sts).

Row 32: k7, skpo, k3, k2tog, k to end (19 sts).

Row 34: k6, skpo, k3, k2tog, k to end (17 sts).

Row 36: k5, skpo, k3, k2tog, k to end (15 sts).

Row 38: k4, skpo, k3, k2tog, k to end (13 sts).

Row 40: k3, skpo, k3, k2tog, k to end (11 sts).

Row 42: k2, skpo, k3, k2tog, k to end (9 sts).

Row 44: k1, skpo, k3, k2tog, k to end (7 sts).
Cut yarn and thread tail through rem sts.

Detail of the wing.

Beak

Using 3.25mm (UK 10; US 3) needles and a single strand of yarn B, cast on 3 sts.

Row 1: p to end.

Row 2: (k1, M1) twice, k1 (5 sts).

Row 3: p to end.

Row 4: k1, M1, k to last st, M1, k1 (2 sts inc).

Next rows: Rep rows 3 and 4 twice more (11 sts).

Row 11: p to end
Cast off.

Detail of the tuft on the head.

To make up

1 Pull up tail of yarn to gather the stitches at the top of the cover. Fold the cover in half with right sides together and stitch the side edges together with a backstitch seam (alternatively, stitch seam from right side using mattress stitch). Turn the cover right side out.

2 Pull up the stitches to gather the top end of each Wing, then stitch one on each side of the cover.

3 Stitch the Beak in place.

4 Cut two circles of felt, approximately 25mm (1in) in diameter and cut a small hole in the centre of each circle. Insert an eye through one of the felt circles, then insert through the knitted fabric and fix in place; repeat for the other eye.

5 Make a bundle of yarn A, tie it around the middle and stitch or tie on top of the head.

The safety eyes sit on small decorative circles of felt.

EAGLE

EAGLE COVER

If you manage to score two under par, you have scored an 'eagle'. That's one better than a birdie! The term crossed the Atlantic from the USA to Britain in 1919.

Measurements and sizes

To fit a driver. This cover measures 14.5cm (50¾in) long; 30cm (12in) circumference at widest part.

YOU WILL NEED

- 50g of DK (light worsted/8-ply) yarn in ivory (A), black (B) and yellow (C). Choose a double knitting yarn that knits to a standard DK (light worsted/8-ply) tension.
- Needles: 3.25mm (UK 10; US 3) and 4mm (UK 8; US 6)
- Tapestry needle
- Sewing needle
- Locking stitch marker
- Stitch holder or safety pin
- Toy stuffing
- Two 12mm (½in) sew-on googly eyes
- White sewing thread

TENSION

20 sts and 26 rows to 10cm (4in), measured over stocking stitch using 4mm (UK 8; US 6) needles, with two strands of yarn.

Detail of the front of the beak.

Detail of the neck.

KNITTING THE COVER

Be aware that one strand of yarn is used for the ribbed part of the cover, and two strands of yarn for the head.

Head

Using 4mm (UK 8; US 6) needles and two strands of yarn A, *cast on 6 sts, cast off 4 sts, transfer st from RH to LH needle; rep from * until there are 48 sts on the needle.

Beg with a knit (RS) row, work 6 rows in st st; place a locking stitch marker on the last row worked.

Row 7: k1, kfb, k20, skpo, k2tog, k20, kfb, k1.

Row 8: p to end.

Rep rows 7 and 8 six times more.

Beg with a k RS row, work 10 rows in st st.

Row 31: (k6, k2tog) three times, (skpo, k6) three times (42 sts).

Row 32 and every WS row: p to end.

Row 33: (k5, k2tog) three times, (skpo, k5) three times (36 sts).

Row 35: (k4, k2tog) three times, (skpo, k4) three times (30 sts).

Row 37: (k3, k2tog) three times, (skpo, k3) three times (24 sts).

Row 39: (k1, k2tog) four times, (skpo, k1) four times (16 sts).

Row 40: (p2tog tbl) four times, (p2tog) four times (8 sts).

Cast off.

Neck

With WS facing and cast-on edge uppermost, using 3.25mm (UK 10; US 3) needles and a single strand of yarn B, pick up and knit 48 sts along marked row.

Work 40 rows of k1, p1 rib.

Cast off loosely in rib.

Beak

The curved shape of the beak is achieved with short-row shaping: knitting or purling a number of stitches along a row, then turning the work before reaching the end of the row. To avoid creating a hole in the fabric, before you turn, slip the next stitch on to the RH needle, wrapping the yarn around the stitch as you do so, then slip it back on to the LH needle. When you pass a wrapped stitch on a following row, knit or purl the stitch together with its wrap.

Using 3.25mm (UK 10; US 3) needles and a single strand of yarn C, cast on 3 sts.

Row 1: p to end.

Row 2: (k1, M1) twice, k1 (5 sts).

Row 3: p to end.

Row 4: k1, M1, k to last st, M1, k1 (7 sts).

Rep rows 3 and 4 three times more (13 sts).

Row 11: p to end.

Row 12: k1, M1, k10, turn.

Row 13: p10, turn.

Row 14: k9, turn.

Row 15: p8, turn.

Row 16: k7, turn.

Row 17: p6, turn.

Row 18: k5, turn.

Row 19: p4, turn.

Row 20: k to last st, M1, k1 (15 sts).

Row 21: p to end.

Row 22: k1, M1, k to last st, M1, k1 (17 sts).

Repeat rows 21 and 22 six times (29 sts).

Beg with a p row, work 3 rows in st st.

Divide beak

Row 1: k1, skpo, k7, k2tog, k1, turn and leave rem sts on a holder (11 sts).

Row 2: p to end.

Row 3: k1, skpo, k5, k2tog, k1 (9 sts).

Row 4: p to end.

Row 5: k1, skpo, k3, k2tog, k1 (7 sts).

Row 6: p to end.

Row 7: k1, skpo, k1, k2tog, k1 (5 sts).

Row 8: p to end.

Row 9: k1, k3tog, k1 (3 sts).

Row 10: p3tog and fasten off.
With RS facing, rejoin yarn to sts on holder, cast off 3 sts, skpo, k to last 3 sts, k2tog, k1 (11 sts).
Work to match first side.

Eye (make 2)

Using 3.25mm (UK 10; US 3) needles and a single strand of yarn C, cast on 6 sts.

Row 1: kfb to end (12 sts).

Row 2: p to end.
Cast off.

To make up

1 Fold cover in half with right sides together and stitch side edges of Head together with a backstitch seam.

2 Stitch seam on Neck. Turn right side out.

3 Stitch seam on Beak and add stuffing but do not overstuff.

4 Pin Beak to front of Head, with one flap on either side; stitch in place.

5 Stitch one Eye piece on either side of head, and stitch a googly eye to the centre of each one.

6 With black yarn, embroider a single chain stitch on each side of the Beak for nostrils.

STARS & STRIPES COVER SET

Major US golf championship tournaments, such as the Masters, the Open and the PGA, are followed with interest by golfing fans worldwide. Introduce a trans-Atlantic vibe to your golf bag with this trio of covers, inspired by the American flag. You can pretend – depending on your age – that you can play as well as luminaries of the tournaments like Jack Nicklaus, Arnold Palmer, Tom Watson or Tiger Woods.

Measurements and sizes

The instructions given are for a cover to fit a 5-wood, with instructions for the larger 3-wood and driver covers given in brackets.

YOU WILL NEED

- 100g of cotton DK (light worsted/8-ply) yarn in white (A), red (B) and blue (C). Choose a double knitting yarn that knits to a standard DK (light worsted/8-ply) tension.; you will need one 100g ball of each of the three colours, or two 50g balls. You could use a wool yarn, or wool blend instead, if you prefer.
- Needles: 3.25mm (UK 10; US 3) and 4mm (UK 8; US 6)
- Tapestry needle

TENSION

20 sts and 26 rows to 10cm (4in), measured over stocking stitch using 4mm (UK 8; US 6) needles, with two strands of yarn.

KNITTING THE COVERS

Follow the pattern for the basic cover on page 18.

For the ribbed section, cast on using 3.25mm (UK 10; US 3) needles and yarn A, and alternate with yarn B to create 2-row stripes.

For the head section, use 4mm (UK 8; US 6) needles and yarn C used double.

To make up

After following the making-up instructions for the basic cover on page 18, thread a tapestry needle with a single strand of yarn A and embroider evenly-spaced stars using overlapping straight stitches, referring to the photographs of the finished covers for guidance.

Land of the Free

As well as having golfing associations, the eagle is a symbol of the USA – so it makes a great focal piece to accompany the Stars & Stripes set.

FUZZY COVER SET

Having the nickname 'Fuzzy' doesn't have to be a handicap... American golfer Frank Urban Zoeller (F.U.Z.) has won ten PGA Tour events, including two major championships and is one of three golfers to have won the Masters Tournament in their first appearance in the event. He first picked up a golf club when he was three, and he played his first competitive tournament – the Junior Falls Cities championship – when he was just five. In his honour, here is a set of three covers made in a delightfully tactile 'fuzzy' yarn.

Eyelash yarn is a novelty yarn with long strands woven into the main strand at even intervals that stick out, creating a furry or 'fuzzy' effect. It creates a soft, furry knitted fabric and is fun to use, though sometimes frustrating as it is not easy to distinguish individual stitch loops and therefore difficult count the stitches and rows.

Measurements and sizes

The instructions given are for a cover to fit a 5-wood, with instructions for the larger 3-wood and driver covers given in brackets.

YOU WILL NEED

- 50g of eyelash yarn in red (A), yellow (B) and blue (C). Choose an eyelash yarn that knits to a standard DK (light worsted/8-ply) tension.
- Needles: 3.25mm (UK 10; US 3) and 4mm (UK 8; US 6)
- Tapestry needle
- Cord elastic
- Wooden beads

TENSION

20 sts and 26 rows to 10cm (4in), measured over stocking stitch using 4mm (UK 8; US 6) needles, with two strands of yarn.

KNITTING THE COVERS

Note that the yarn is used single for the ribbed part of the cover, and double for the top part.

Using 3.25mm (UK10; US3) needles, cast on 24 (30, 36) sts.

Row 1: *k1, p1; rep from * to end of row.
Rep row 1 23 (29, 35) times.

Next row (eyelets): k1, *yfwd, k2tog; rep from * to last st, k1.

Next row: *k1, p1; rep from * to end of row.
Change to 4mm (UK 8; US 6) needles and two strands of yarn.

Row 1: k.

Row 2: p.

Row 3: (k5, kfb) 4 (5, 6) times. 28 (35, 42) sts.

Row 4: p.

Row 5: (k6, kfb) 4 (5, 6) times. 32 (40, 48) sts.
Beg with a p row, work 11 (15, 19) rows st st.
Shape top.

Row 1: (k6, k2tog) 4 (5, 6) times. 28 (35, 42) sts.

Row 2 (and every even-numbered row): p.

Row 3: (k5, k2tog) 4 (5, 6) times. 24 (30, 36) sts.

Row 5: (k4, k2tog) 4 (5, 6) times. 20 (35, 30) sts.

Row 7: (k3, k2tog) 4 (5, 6) times. 16 (20, 24) sts.

Row 9: (k2, k2tog) 4 (5, 6) times. 12 (15, 18) sts.

Row 11: (k1, k2tog) 4 (5, 6) times. 8 (10, 12) sts.

Row 12: (p2tog) 4 (5, 6) times.
Cut yarn, leaving a long tail, and thread tail through rem sts.

To make up

1 Pull up tail of yarn to gather stitches at top of cover. Fold cover in half with right sides together and stitch side edges together with a backstitch seam.

2 Turn right sides out. Cut a 34 (36, 38)cm (13½/14¼/15in) length of cord elastic and thread through the eyelet holes.

3 Thread both ends of the elastic through the hole in a wooden bead, then knot the elastic ends together.

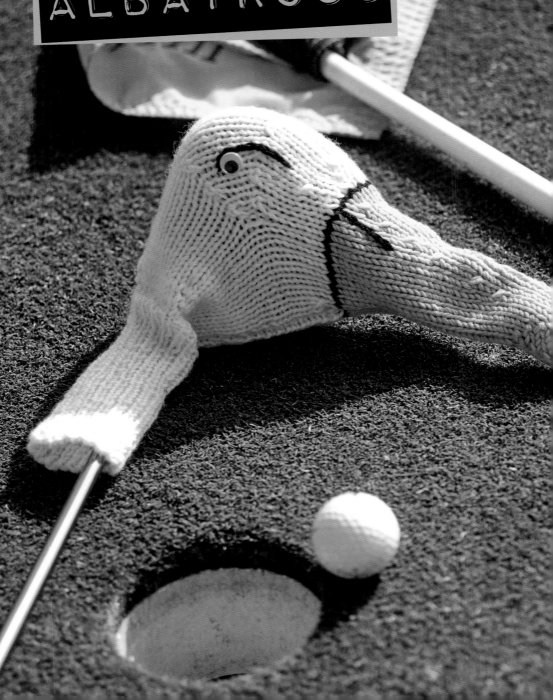

ALBATROSS

ALBATROSS COVER

Surely every golfer dreams of achieving three strokes under par on a hole? This is a very difficult score to achieve – and so in golf circles such as score is referred to as an 'albatross', in reference to the equally rare sightings of this enormous bird.

While 'birdie' and 'eagle' are American in origin, the term 'albatross' probably began in Britain in the 1920s. To celebrate its rarity, this knitted albatross, unlike most of the covers in this book, has a curved shape and will fit a range of different clubs, including a putter.

Measurements and sizes

To fit a range of different clubs. This cover measures 40cm (16in) long; 25cm (10in) circumference at widest part.

YOU WILL NEED

- 50g of DK (light worsted/8-ply) yarn in ivory (A) and mustard (C) and a small amount of black (B). Choose a double knitting yarn that knits to a standard DK (light worsted/8-ply) tension.
- Needles: 3.25mm (UK 10; US 3) and 4mm (UK 8; US 6)
- Tapestry needle
- Sewing needle
- Two 12mm (½in) sew-on googly eyes
- White sewing thread

TENSION

20 sts and 26 rows to 10cm (4in), measured over stocking stitch using 4mm (UK 8; US 6) needles, with two strands of yarn.

KNITTING THE COVER

Neck

Using 3.25mm (UK 10; US 3) needles and a single strand of yarn A, cast on 32 sts and work 40 rows in k1, p1 rib.

Head

Change to 4mm (UK 8; US 6) needles and use two strands of yarn A.

Row 1 (RS): k to end.

Row 2 (WS): p to end.

Row 3: (k7, kfb) twice, (kfb, k7) twice (36 sts).

Row 4: p to end.

Row 5: (k8, kfb) twice, (kfb, k8) twice (40 sts).

Beg with a p row, work 13 rows in st st.

Row 19: k30, turn.

Row 20: p20, turn.

Row 21: k18, turn.

Row 22: p16, turn.

Row 23: k14, turn.

Row 24: p12, turn.

Row 25: k10, turn.

Row 26: p8, turn.

Row 27: k10, turn.

Row 28: p12, turn.

Row 29: k14, turn.

Row 30: p16, turn.

Row 31: k18, turn.

Row 32: p20, turn.

Row 33: k to end.

Row 34: p to end.

Rep rows 19–33 once more.

Beg with a p row, work 3 rows in st st.

Row 53: k12, (skpo, k2) twice, (k2, k2tog) twice, k to end (36 sts).

Row 54: p to end.

Row 55: k1, skpo, k11, skpo, k4, k2tog, k to last 3 sts, k2tog, k1 (32 sts).

Row 56: p to end; fasten off yarn A and join in yarn B.

Row 57: k12, skpo, k4, k2tog, k to end; fasten off yarn B and join in yarn C (30 sts).

Beg with a p row, work 3 rows in st st.

Row 61: k11, skpo, k4, k2tog, k to end (28 sts).

Beg with a p row, work 3 rows in st st.

Row 65: k10, skpo, k4, k2tog, k to end (26 sts).

Beg with a p row, work 3 rows in st st.

Row 69: k9, skpo, k4, k2tog, k to end (24 sts).

Row 70: p to end.

Row 71: k9, skpo, k2, k2tog, k to end (22 sts).

Row 72: p to end.

Row 73: k8, skpo, k2, k2tog, k to end (20 sts).

Beg with a p row, work 5 rows in st st.

Row 79: k7, skpo, k2, k2tog, k to end (18 sts).

Beg with a p row, work 3 rows in st st.

Row 83: k6, skpo, k2, k2tog, k to end (16 sts).

Row 84: p to end.

Row 85: k14, turn.

Row 86: p12, turn.

Row 87: k11, turn.

Row 88: p10, turn.

Row 89: k9, turn.

Row 90: p8, turn.

Row 91: k7, turn.

Row 92: p6, turn.

Row 93: k to end.

Row 94: p1, p2tog, p to last 3 sts, p2tog tbl, p1 (14 sts).

Row 95: k to end.

Rep rows 94 and 95 once (12 sts).

Row 98: as row 94 (10 sts).

Row 99: k1, skpo, k4, k2tog, k1 (8 sts).

Row 100: as row 94 (6 sts).

Row 101: k1, skpo, k2tog, k1 (4 sts).

Row 102: p1, p2tog, p1 (3 sts). Cast off.

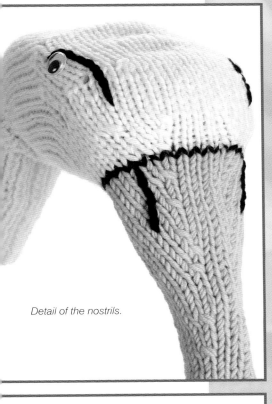

Detail of the nostrils.

To make up

1 Fold the cover in half, with right sides together and stitch side edges together with a backstitch seam. Turn right side out.

2 Sew googly eyes in place, one on each side of head.

3 With black yarn, embroider a curved line of chain stitch above each eye and a straight line of chain stitch on each side of the beak.

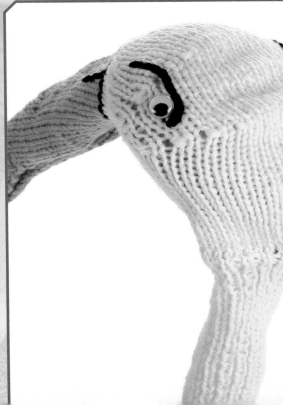

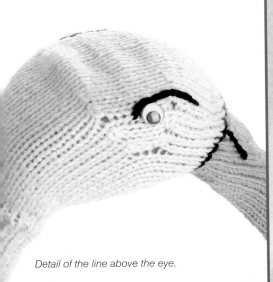

Detail of the line above the eye.

BOGEY

BOGEYMAN COVER SET

In the world of golf, a bogey is a score of one above par. It is a shortened form of
bogeyman, a term likely derived from the Scots dialect word 'bogle', which refers
to a goblin or devil. As an incentive for the golfer in your life who hopes to improve
his or her handicap, knit this trio of little demons. Choose your own colour palette
– after all, who can say what colour these little critters should be?

Measurements and sizes

The instructions given are for a cover to fit a 5-wood, with instructions for the
larger 3-wood and driver covers given in brackets.

YOU WILL NEED

- 50g of DK (light worsted/8-ply) yarn
  in blue (A), red (B), ivory (D), jade
  green (E) and black (F), 100g of DK
  (light worsted/8-ply) yarn in ultra
  violet (C). Choose a double knitting
  yarn that knits to a standard DK
  (light worsted/8-ply) tension.
- Needles: 3.25mm (UK 10; US 3), 4mm
  (UK 8; US 6) and two 3.25mm (UK 10;
  US 3) double-pointed needles
- Tapestry needle
- Toy stuffing

TENSION

20 sts and 26 rows to 10cm (4in),
measured over stocking stitch using
4mm (UK 8; US 6) needles, with two
strands of yarn.

KNITTING THE COVERS

Main head

Using yarn A (B, C), follow the pattern for the basic cover.

Ear (make 2: 5-wood and driver only)

Using 3.25mm (UK 10; US 3) needles and a single strand of yarn A (C), cast on 13 (21) sts and knit 21 (31) rows.

**Next row: k1, k2tog, k to last 3 sts, k2tog, k1 (2 sts dec).

Next rows: Knit 3 (5) rows**.
Rep from ** to ** until 5 sts rem.

Next row: k1, sl1, k2tog, psso, k1 (3 sts).

Next row: sl1, k2tog, psso and fasten off.

Devil Horn (make 2: 3-wood only)

Using 3.25mm (UK 10; US 3) needles and a single strand of yarn B, cast on 3 sts.

Row 1: k to end.

Row 2: (k1, M1) twice, k1 (5 sts).

Row 3: k2, p1, k2.

Row 4: k2, M1, k1, M1, k2 (7 sts).

Row 5: k2, p to last 2 sts, k2.

Row 6: k2, M1, k to last 2 sts, M1, k2 (2 sts inc).
Rep rows 5 and 6 seven times (23 sts).

Row 21: k2, p to last 2 sts, k2.

Row 22: k to end.
Rep rows 21 and 22 six times.
Cast off pwise.

Teeth

Using 3.25mm (UK 10; US 3) needles and a single strand of yarn D, cast on 11 (15, 19) sts.

Row 1: p to end.

Row 2: kfb, k to last st, kfb (2 sts inc).
Rep rows 1 and 2 once (15, 19, 23 sts).
Beg with a p row, work 3 (5, 7) rows in st st.

Next row: k2tog, k to last 2 sts, k2tog (2 sts dec).

Next row: p to end.
Rep last two rows once more (11, 15, 19 sts).
Cast off.

Lips

Using two 3.25mm (UK 10; US 3) double-pointed needles and a single strand of yarn A (B, C), cast on 2 (3, 4) sts.

Row 1: k2 (3, 4); do not turn but slide sts to end of needle.
Rep row 1 until i-cord is long enough to fit around the perimeter of the Teeth. Cut yarn and fasten off.

Eyeball (make 2)

Using 3.25mm (UK 10; US 3) needles and a single strand of yarn D, cast on 6 (8, 10) sts.

Row 1: kfb in each st (12, 16, 20 sts).

Row 2: p to end.
Cast off.

Iris (make 2)

Using 3.25mm (UK 10; US 3) needles and a single strand of yarn E, cast on 6 sts.

Row 1: kfb to end (12 sts).

Row 2: k to end.
Cut yarn and thread through all sts.

Nose

Using 3.25mm (UK 10; US 3) needles and a single strand of yarn A (B, C), cast on 6 (8, 10) sts.

Row 1: kfb to end (12 (16, 20) sts).

Row 2: p to end.

Row 3: (k1, kfb) to end (18 (24, 30) sts).

Row 4: p to end.
Cast off.

To make up

1 Fold cover in half with right sides together and stitch side edges together. Turn right side out.

2 Stitch the ears in place. For the Devil Horns, stitch the side seam, stuff, then pin the cast-on edge of each in place on either side of the head. Stitch in place.

3 Stitch the seams on the Eyeballs and Irises, then stitch them in place. Embroider the centre of the eyes using yarn F and satin stitch.

4 Using yarn F, embroider a curved line of chain stitch for each eyebrow and a straight line of backstitch across the centre of the Teeth.

5 Stitch the lips in place.

6 Roll up the nose tightly, to form a cone, then stitch in place.

Detail of the horn.

SNOWMAN FAMILY COVER SET

A dedicated golfer will play in all weathers, so here is a family of snow people to protect clubs when the weather turns a bit frosty.

Measurements and sizes

The instructions given are for a cover to fit a 5-wood, with instructions for the larger 3-wood and driver covers given in brackets.

YOU WILL NEED

- 100g of DK (light worsted/8-ply) yarn in snowy white (A), 50g in black (B), bright pink (C) and cornflower blue (D), and small amounts of orange (E) and green (F). Choose a double knitting yarn that knits to a standard DK (light worsted/8-ply) tension. The yarn used for these snow people is 100% acrylic.
- Needles: 3.25mm (UK 10; US 3) and 4mm (UK 8; US 6)
- Tapestry needle

TENSION

22 sts and 30 rows to 10cm (4in), measured over stocking stitch using 4mm (UK 8; US 6) needles, with a single strand of yarn.

KNITTING THE COVERS

Body

Using 3.25mm (UK 10; US 3) needles and yarn A, follow the pattern for the basic cover in all three sizes, changing to 4mm (UK 8; US 6) needles and yarn held double as indicated.

Head

Using 3.25mm (UK 10; US 3) needles and a single strand of yarn A, cast on 10 (12, 12) sts.

Row 1: p to end.

Row 2: (k1, kfb) to end (15 (18, 18) sts).

Row 3: p to end.

Row 4: (k2, kfb) to end (20 (24, 24) sts).

Row 5: p to end.

Row 6: (k3, kfb) to end (25 (30, 30) sts).
Beg with a p row, work 5 (5,7) rows in st st.

Next row: (k3, k2tog) to end (20 (24, 24) sts).

Next row: p to end.

Next row: (k2, k2tog) to end (15 (18, 18) sts).

Next row: p to end.

Next row: (k1, k2tog) to end (10 (12, 12) sts).
Cut yarn and thread through all sts.

Scarf

Using 3.25mm (UK 10; US 3) needles and a single strand of yarn C (D, C), cast on 8 (10, 12) sts.

Work in k1, p1 rib until work measures 32 (35, 38)cm (12½ (13¾, 15)in), alternating with yarn F every 2 rows for the striped version.

Coal Eyes and Buttons (make 5 small, 5 medium, 5 large)

Using 3.25mm (UK 10; US 3) needles and a single strand of yarn B, cast on 4 (5, 6) sts.

Row 1: kfb to end (8 (10, 12) sts).
Cut yarn and thread through all sts.

Nose

Using 3.25mm (UK 10; US 3) needles and a single strand of yarn E, cast on 3 sts.

Row 1 and every WS row: p to end.

Row 2: kfb to end (6 sts).

Row 4: kfb to end (12 sts).

Row 6: (k1, kfb) to end (18 sts).

Row 8: (k2, kfb) to end (24 sts).
Cast off.

Bobble Hat

Using 3.25mm (UK 10; US 3) needles and a single strand of yarn C, cast on 36 sts.

Work in k1, p1 rib for 10 rows. Change to 4mm (UK 8; US 6) needles.

Row 11 (RS): k to end.

Row 12 (WS): p to end; do not cut yarn but join in F.

Row 13: using yarn F, k to end.

Row 14 and every WS row: p to end.

Row 15: using yarn C, (k4, k2tog) to end (30 sts).

Row 17: using yarn F, (k3, k2tog) to end (24 sts).

Row 19: using yarn C, (k2, k2tog) to end (18 sts).

Row 21: using yarn F, (k1, k2tog) to end (12 sts).

Row 22: (p2tog) to end (6 sts).
Cut yarn and thread through rem sts.

Black Hat Crown

Using 3.25mm (UK 10; US 3) needles and a single strand of yarn B, cast on 40 sts.

Knit 16 rows.

Row 17: (k3, k2tog) to end (32 sts).

Details of the hats.

Row 18: (k2, k2tog) to end (24 sts).

Row 19: (k1, k2tog) to end (16 sts).

Row 20: (k2tog) to end (8 sts).

Row 21: (k2tog) to end (4 sts).

Cut yarn and thread through rem sts.

Black Hat Brim

Using 3.25mm (UK 10; US 3) needles and a single strand of yarn B, cast on 40 sts.

Row 1: k to end.

Row 2: (k4, kfb) to end (48 sts).

Row 3: (k5, kfb) to end (56 sts).

Row 4: (k6, kfb) to end (64 sts).

Row 5: (k7, kfb) to end (72 sts).

Row 6: (k8, kfb) to end (80 sts).

Knit 2 rows.

Cast off.

Headband

Using 3.25mm (UK 10; US 3) needles and yarn C, cast on 36 sts.

Beg with a p row, work 5 rows in st st.

Cast off.

To make up

1 Pull up tail of yarn to gather stitches at top of cover. Fold cover in half with right sides together and stitch side edges together with a backstitch seam (alternatively, stitch seam from right side using mattress stitch). Turn right side out.

2 Stitch side seam on the Head and pull up tail of yarn on top, to close.

3 Stuff, then stitch open (cast-on) edge to top of cover.

4 Pull up yarn tightly on each piece of 'Coal' and form into a rough ball shape, then stitch each one in place on Head and Cover, to represent eyes and buttons.

5 Roll up Nose tightly into a cone shape – adding a little stuffing to the largest size to make it bigger – and stitch each one to the front of each Head.

6 Stitch seam on Bobble Hat and pull up tail of yarn on top, to close. Make a small pompom using yarn C and stitch to top.

7 For Black Hat, stitch seam on Crown and pull up tail of yarn on top, then stitch seam on Brim and attach to Crown.

8 Join short ends of Headband; make a small pompom using yarn D and stitch in place to cover join.

PANDAS

GIANT PANDA COVER SET

This panda family represents a rare phenomenon, as the giant panda is notoriously reluctant to breed in captivity and the species is threatened by extinction in the wild. The rarity of this trio will therefore be a good talking point on the golf course or the clubhouse – besides which, it should definitely appeal to the golfer who likes a matching set, or who prefers monochrome to bright colours.

Measurements and sizes

As for the basic cover on page 16. The instructions given are for a cover to fit a 5-wood, with instructions for the larger 3-wood and driver covers given in brackets.

YOU WILL NEED

- 100g of DK (light worsted/8-ply) yarn in black (A) and ivory (B). Choose a double knitting yarn that knits to a standard DK (light worsted/8-ply) tension.
- Needles: 3.25mm (UK 10; US 3) and 4mm (UK 8; US 6)
- Tapestry needle
- Toy safety eyes, brown: 1 pair 12mm (½in), 2 pairs 8mm (⅜in)
- Toy stuffing

TENSION

22 sts and 30 rows to 10cm (4in), measured over stocking stitch using 4mm (UK 8; US 6) needles, with single strand of yarn.

KNITTING THE COVERS

Yarn is used singly unless otherwise stated. Follow the pattern for the basic cover (see page 18) for all three sizes, using yarn A for the ribbed section (using a single strand of yarn) and yarn B for the head (using two strands of yarn).

Eye Patches (make 2)

Using 3.25mm (UK 10; US 3) needles and yarn A, cast on 2 (4, 6) sts.

Row 1 (WS): p to end.

Row 2 (RS): kfb, k to last st, kfb (2 sts inc).
Rep rows 1 and 2 once more (6 (8, 10) sts).
Beg with a p row, work 1 (3, 5) rows in st st.

Next row: k2tog, k to last 2 sts, k2tog (2 sts dec).

Next row: p to end.
Rep last 2 rows 1 (2, 2) times more.
Cast off.

Ear (make 4)

Using 3.25mm (UK 10; US 3) needles and yarn A, cast on 10 (12, 16) sts.

Row 1 (RS): k each st tbl.
Beg with a p row, work 7 (9, 11) rows in st st.

Next row: k1, skpo, k to last 3 sts, k2tog, k1 (2 sts dec).

Next row: p to end.
Rep the last 2 rows 1 (2, 3) times more (6 (6, 8) sts).
Cast off.

Nose

Using 3.25mm (UK 10; US 3) needles and yarn A, cast on 2 sts.

Row 1 (WS): p to end.

Row 2 (RS): kfb twice (4 sts).

Row 3: p to end.

Row 4: kfb, k to last st, kfb (2 sts inc).
Rep rows 3 and 4 2 (3, 4) times more (10 (12, 14) sts).
Beg with a p row, work 1 (3, 5) rows in st st.
Cast off.

To make up

1 Pull up tail of yarn to gather stitches at top of cover. Fold cover in half with right sides together and stitch side edges together with a backstitch seam (alternatively, stitch seam from right side using mattress stitch). Turn right side out.

2 Stitch Eye Patches in place, then insert a safety eye into each one and use washers to lock securely in place on the reverse.

3 Place two Ears right sides together and stitch together round curved edge, leaving cast-on edge unstitched. Turn right sides out and stitch open edge to side of head.

4 Gather cast-off edge of Nose slightly and stitch Nose in place, adding a tiny bit of stuffing to pad out shape.

Detail of the stitching on the face.

SNAKE CHARMER

SNAKE COVER

This slithery customer covers not only the head but most of the shaft of your 3-wood. Choose your own combination of colours to work the stripes. The yarn shades used here were inspired by the bright stripes of the coral snake and the less dangerous corn snake – but you could perhaps substitute your club colours to good effect.

Measurements and sizes

The instructions given are for a cover to fit a 3-wood.

YOU WILL NEED

- 50g of acrylic DK (light worsted/8-ply) yarn in orange (A), black (B) and white (C), and small amount of red (D). Choose a double knitting yarn that knits to a standard DK (light worsted/8-ply) tension. The acrylic yarn used here was chosen for its vivid colours.
- Needles: 3.25mm (UK 10; US 3) and 4mm (UK 8; US 6)
- Tapestry needle

TENSION

22 sts and 30 rows to 10cm (4in), measured over stocking stitch using 4mm (UK 8; US 6) needles, with single strand of yarn.

KNITTING THE COVER

Be aware that one strand of yarn is used for the ribbed part of the cover, and two strands of yarn for the head.

Body and Head (in one piece)

Using 3.25mm (UK 10; US 3) needles and yarn A, cast on 30 sts.

Row 1 (WS): (k1, p1) to end.
Rep row 1 twice more; do not cut yarn A but join in yarn B.
Using yarn B, rep row 1 twice; do not cut yarn B but join in yarn C.
Using yarn C, rep row 1 four times.
Using yarn B, rep row 1 twice.
Using yarn A, rep row 1 eight times.
Continue like this, working in stripes, until you have worked 11 banded white stripes and 11 orange stripes.
Fasten off yarns B and C, change to 4mm (UK 8; US 6) needles and continue in yarn A only for the head, using two strands of yarn.

Head

Row 1 (RS): k to end.

Row 2: p to end.

Row 3: (k4, kfb) to end (36 sts).

Row 4: p to end.

Row 5: (k5, kfb) to end (42 sts).
Beg with a p row, work 19 rows in st st.

Row 25: (k4, k2tog) to end (35 sts).

Row 26: p to end.

Row 27: (k3, k2tog) to end (28 sts).

Row 28: p to end.

Row 29: (k2, k2tog) to end (21 sts).

Row 30: p to end.

Row 31: (k1, k2tog) to end (14 sts).

Row 32: (p2tog) to end (7 sts).
Cut yarn and thread tail through rem sts.

Eyeball (make 2)

Using 3.25mm (UK 10; US 3) needles and a single strand of yarn C, cast on 6 sts.

Row 1: k to end.

Row 2: kfb, k to last st, kfb (2 sts inc).
Rep rows 1 and 2 once more (10 sts).
Knit 5 rows.

Row 10: k2tog, k to last 2 sts, k2tog (2 sts dec).

Row 11: k to end.
Rep rows 10 and 11 once more (6 sts).
Cast off.

Pupil (make 2)

Using 3.25mm (UK 10; US 3) needles and a single strand of yarn B, cast on 6 sts.

Row 1: k to end.

Row 2: kfb, k to last st, kfb (2 sts inc).
Rep rows 1 and 2 once more (10 sts).

Row 5: k to end

Row 6: k2tog, k to last 2 sts, k2tog (2 sts dec).

Row 7: k to end.
Rep rows 6 and 7 once more (6 sts).
Cast off.

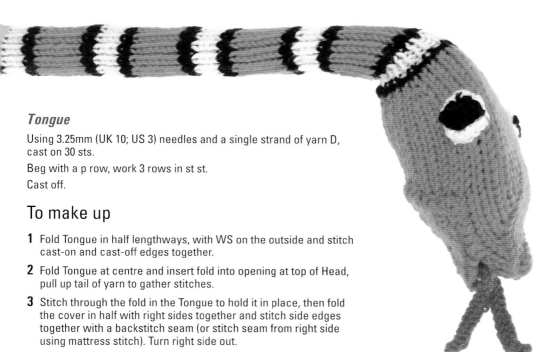

Tongue

Using 3.25mm (UK 10; US 3) needles and a single strand of yarn D, cast on 30 sts.

Beg with a p row, work 3 rows in st st.

Cast off.

To make up

1 Fold Tongue in half lengthways, with WS on the outside and stitch cast-on and cast-off edges together.

2 Fold Tongue at centre and insert fold into opening at top of Head, pull up tail of yarn to gather stitches.

3 Stitch through the fold in the Tongue to hold it in place, then fold the cover in half with right sides together and stitch side edges together with a backstitch seam (or stitch seam from right side using mattress stitch). Turn right side out.

4 Stitch Eyes in place, with Pupils in centre.

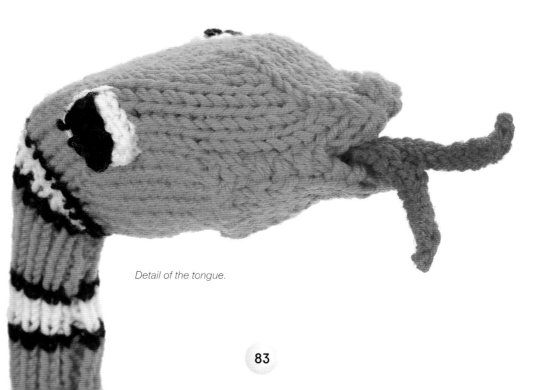

Detail of the tongue.

FROGS

FROG PRINCE AND PRINCESS COVER SET

Knitted in green yarn, to blend in with the grass on the golf course, here is a pair of frogs. They are wearing crowns, which would suggest they are, perhaps, a frog prince and princess, waiting to be kissed? Try it and see what happens: they may bring a stroke of luck.

Measurements and sizes

The Frog Prince cover will fit a driver, while the Frog Princess will fit a 3-wood.

TENSION

22 sts and 30 rows to 10cm (4in), measured over stocking stitch using 4mm (UK 8; US 6) needles, with single strand of yarn.

KNITTING THE COVERS

Be aware that, for the larger size, one strand of yarn is used for the ribbed part of the cover, and two strands of yarn for the head; for the smaller size, follow the same pattern but use a single strand of yarn throughout.

Frog (in one piece)

Neck

Using 3.25mm (UK 10; US 3) needles and a single strand of yarn A, cast on 36 sts.

Work 36 rows in k1, p1 rib.

Larger size only: change to 4mm (UK 8; US 6) needles and use two strands of yarn.

Head

Row 1 (RS): k to end.

Row 2 (WS): p to end.

Row 3: (k5, kfb) to end (42 sts).

Row 4: p to end.

Row 5: (k6, kfb) to end (48 sts).
Beg with a p row, work 21 rows in st st.

Row 27: (k10, k2tog) to end (44 sts).

Row 28 and every WS row: p to end.

Row 29: (k9, k2tog) to end (40 sts).

Row 31: (k6, k2tog) to end (35 sts).

Row 33: (k5, k2tog) to end (30 sts).

Row 35: (k3, k2tog) to end (24 sts).

Row 37: (k1, k2tog) to end (16 sts).

Row 38: (p2tog) to end (8 sts).

Row 39: (k2tog) to end (4 sts).
Cut yarn and thread through rem sts.

Pupil (make 2)

Using 3.25mm (UK 10; US 3) needles and a single strand of yarn B, cast on 6 sts.

Row 1: k to end.

Row 2: kfb, k to last st, kfb (2 sts inc).
Rep rows 1 and 2 once more (10 sts).

Row 5: k to end

Row 6: k2tog, k to last 2 sts, k2tog (2 sts dec).

Row 7: k to end.
Rep rows 6 and 7 once more (6 sts).
Cast off.

Eyeball, small (make 2)

Using 3.25mm (UK 10; US 3) needles and a single strand of yarn C, cast on 6 sts.

Row 1 (RS): kfb to end (12 sts).

Row 2 and every WS row: p to end.

Row 3: (k1, kfb) to end (18 sts).

Row 5: (k2, kfb) to end (24 sts).

Row 7: (k3, kfb) to end (30 sts).

Row 9: (k3, k2tog) to end (24 sts).

Row 11: (k2, k2tog) to end (18 sts).

Row 13: (k1, k2tog) to end (12 sts).

Row 15: (k2tog) to end (6 sts).
Cut yarn and thread through rem sts.

Eyeball, large (make 2)

Follow instructions for small Eyeball to the end of row 7.

Row 8 (WS): p to end.

Row 9 (RS): (k4, kfb) to end (36 sts).

Row 10: p to end.

Row 11: (k5, kfb) to end (42 sts).

Row 12: p to end.

Row 13: (k5, k2tog) to end (36 sts).

Row 14: p to end.

Row 15: (k4, k2tog) to end (30 sts).
Follow instructions for small Eyeball from row 9 to end.

Eye Socket, small (make 2)

Using 3.25mm (UK 10; US 3) needles and a single strand of yarn A, cast on 6 sts.

Row 1 (RS): kfb to end (12 sts).

Row 2 and every WS row: p to end.

Row 3: (k1, kfb) to end (18 sts).

Row 5: (k2, kfb) to end (24 sts).

Row 7: (k3, kfb) to end (30 sts).

Row 9: k to end.

Row 10: p to end.
Cast off.

Eye Socket, large (make 2)

Follow instructions for small Eye Socket to the end of row 7.

Row 8 (WS): p to end.

Row 9 (RS): (k4, kfb) to end (36 sts).

Row 10: p to end.

Row 11: (k5, kfb) to end (42 sts).

Row 12: p to end.

Row 13: (k5, k2tog) to end (36 sts).

Row 14: p to end.

Row 15: k to end.
Cast off.

Crown, both sizes

Using 3.25mm (UK 10; US 3) needles and a single strand of yarn B, cast on 12 sts.

Row 1: sl1, k4, p1, k to end.

Row 2: kfb, k to end (13 sts).

Row 3: sl1, k4, k to last st, kfb (14 sts).

Row 4: kfb, k to end (15 sts).

Row 5: sl1, k4, k to last st, kfb (16 sts).

Row 6: kfb, k to end (17 sts).

Row 7: sl1, k4, k to end.

Row 8: k2tog, k to end (16 sts).

Row 9: sl1, k4, k to last st, k2tog (15 sts).

Row 10: k2tog, k to end (14 sts).

Row 11: sl1, k4, k to last st, k2tog (13 sts).

Row 12: k2tog, k to end (12 sts).
Rep rows 1–12 five (six) times more.
Cast off.

Detail of the eye.

Detail of the rear of the crown.

Mouth

Using 3.25mm (UK 10; US 3) needles and a single strand of yarn A, cast on 25 (30) sts.

Beg with a p row, work 3 rows in st st.

Cast off.

To make up

1 Pull up tail of yarn to gather stitches at top of cover. Fold cover in half with right sides together and stitch side edges together with a backstitch seam. Turn right sides out.

2 Stitch seam on Eyeball and Eye Socket, and slip Eyeball inside. Stitch Pupils in place. Stitch to each side of Head.

3 Stitch seam on Crown, then decorate with plastic bobble trim and gems. Stitch Crown to top of Head, in between Eyes.

4 Stitch Mouth in place, curving it into a smile. Using a strand of yarn D, embroider a line of chain stitch along centre of Mouth, then add two single chain stitches for nostrils.

OWLS

OWL COVER SET

During the 2016 Olympics in Rio, an owl caused a bit of a stir on the golf course by making its burrow on the ninth green. Whether you are just having a practice, playing a friendly game, or taking part in a competition, these owls, being made from yarn, are less likely to cause a disruption.

Pompoms have been used elsewhere in the book and you will find instructions for making them on page 13. A similar technique is used for these ear tufts. Here a looser bundle, rather than a full pompom, looks more effective.

Measurements and sizes

As for the basic cover on page 16. The instructions given are for a cover to fit a 5-wood, with instructions for the larger 3-wood and driver covers given in brackets.

YOU WILL NEED

- 100g of DK (light worsted/8-ply) yarn in beige (A), 50g in ivory (B) and yellow (C), and small amount of brown (D). Choose a double knitting yarn that knits to a standard DK (light worsted/8-ply) tension.
- Needles: 3.25mm (UK 10; US 3) and 4mm (UK 8; US 6)
- Three pairs of black buttons, in various sizes
- Toy stuffing

TENSION

20 sts and 26 rows to 10cm (4in), measured over stocking stitch using 4mm (UK 8; US 6) needles, with two strands of yarn.

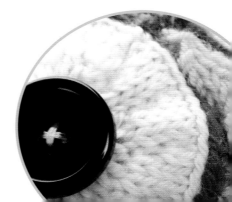

KNITTING THE COVERS

Using 3.25mm (UK 10; US 3) needles and yarn A, follow the pattern for the basic cover (see pages 16–19), for all three sizes, changing to 4mm (UK 8; US 6) needles and yarn held double as indicated.

Eyes, all sizes

Using 3.25mm (UK 10; US 3) needles and yarn B, cast on 6 sts.

Row 1 (RS): kfb to end (12 sts).

Row 2 (WS): p to end.

Row 3: kfb to end (24 sts).

Row 4: p to end.
Cast off for small size only.

Row 5 (med and large only): (k1, kfb) to end (36 sts).

Row 6: p to end.
Cast off for med size.

Row 7 (large only): (k2, kfb) to end (48 sts).

Row 8: p to end.
Cast off for large size.

Beak, all sizes

Using 3.25mm (UK 10; US 3) needles and yarn C, cast on 3 sts.

Row 1 (WS): p to end.

Row 2 (RS): (k1, M1) twice, k1 (5 sts).

Row 3: p to end.

Row 4: k1, M1, k to last st, M1, k1 (2 sts inc).
Rep rows 3 and 4 until there are 9 (13, 17) sts.

Next row: p to end.

Next row: k1, skpo, k to last 3 sts, k2tog, k1 (2 sts dec).

Rep last 2 rows until 5 sts rem.

Next row: p to end.

Next row: skpo, k1, k2tog (3 sts).

Next row: p to end.

Next row: sl1, k2tog, psso and fasten off.

To make up

1 Follow the making-up instructions for the basic cover on page 18.

2 Using leftover yarn, make six loose pompoms or bundles of yarn in various sizes. To make a bundle, wrap yarn around a small rectangle of card (or an object such as a mobile phone, or even a few fingers); slip it off and tie a length of yarn around the middle, then cut through the loops and trim to size.

3 Stitch or tie two bundles firmly to the top of each of the covers, to form ear tufts.

4 Stitch Eyes in place, then thread tapestry needle with a single strand of yarn D and stitch a border of chain stitch around each Eye.

5 Stitch buttons in the centres of the Eyes.

6 Roll up the Beak and stitch to form a cone shape. Stuff lightly and stitch to face, between eyes.

SHARK

SHARK COVER

Australian Greg Norman won more than ninety tournaments worldwide, including two Open Championships, and was inducted into the World Golf Hall of Fame in 2001 with a higher percentage of votes than any other golfer in history. These days he heads a dozen or so companies around the world, bearing his name and the iconic shark logo that refers to his nickname, 'The Great White Shark'. If you're a fan, you'll want this eye-catching cover in your kit.

Measurements and sizes

The instructions given are for a cover to fit a driver. This cover measures 14.5cm (50¾in) long; 30cm (12in) circumference at widest part.

YOU WILL NEED

- 50g of DK (light worsted/8-ply) yarn in grey (A) and red (B). Choose a double knitting yarn that knits to a standard DK (light worsted/8-ply) tension.
- Needles: 3.25mm (UK 10; US 3) and 4mm (UK 8; US 6)
- White felt
- Sewing needle and white thread
- Two black toy safety eyes

TENSION

20 sts and 26 rows to 10cm (4in), measured over stocking stitch using 4mm (UK 8; US 6) needles, with two strands of yarn.

KNITTING THE COVER

Body

Using 3.25mm (UK10; US3) needles and yarn A, cast on 36 sts.

Rows 1–36: (k1, p1) to end.
Change to 4mm (UK 8; US 6) and two strands of yarn A.

Head and Upper Jaw

Row 1 (RS): k18, turn and leave rem sts on a stitch holder.

Row 2: p to end.

Row 3: k1, M1, k7, M1, k2, M1, k7, M1, k1 (22 sts).

Row 4: p to end.

Row 5: k1, M1, k9, M1, k2, M1, k9, M1, k1 (26 sts).

Row 6: p to end.

Row 7: k1, M1, k11, M1, k2, M1, k11, M1, k1 (30 sts).

Row 8: p to end.
Beg with a p row, work 23 rows in st st.

Row 32: k1, skpo, k9, skpo, k2, k2tog, k9, k2tog, k1 (26 sts).

Row 33: p to end.

Row 34: k1, skpo, k7, skpo, k2, k2tog, k7, k2tog, k1 (22 sts).

Row 35: p to end.

Row 36: k1, skpo, k5, skpo, k2, k2tog, k5, k2tog, k1 (18 sts).

Row 37: p to end.

Row 38: k1, skpo, k3, skpo, k2, k2tog, k3, k2tog, k1 (14 sts).

Row 39: p to end.

Row 40: k1, skpo, k1, skpo, k2, k2tog, k1, k2tog, k1 (10 sts).

Row 41: p to end.

Row 42: k1, (skpo) twice, (k2tog) twice, k1 (6 sts).
Cast off purlwise.

Lower Jaw

With RS facing, rejoin two strands of yarn A to held sts.

Row 1 (RS): k to end.

Row 2: p to end.

Row 3: k1, M1, k to last st, M1, k1 (2 sts inc).
Rep rows 2 and 3 twice more (24 sts).
Beg with a p row, work 19 rows in st st.

Row 27: k1, skpo, k6, skpo, k2, k2tog, k6, k2tog, k1 (20 sts).

Row 28: p to end.

Row 29: k1, skpo, k4, skpo, k2, k2tog, k4, k2tog, k1 (16 sts).

Row 30: p to end.

Row 31: k1, skpo, k2, skpo, k2, k2tog, k2, k2tog, k1 (12 sts).

Row 32: p to end.

Row 33: k1, (skpo) twice, k2, (k2tog) twice, k1 (8 sts).

Row 34: k1, sl1, k2tog, psso, k3tog, k1 (4 sts).
Cast off purlwise.

Mouth

Using 4mm (UK 8; US 6) and two strands of yarn B, cast on 2 sts.

Row 1 (WS): p to end.

Row 2 (RS): kfb twice (4 sts).

Row 3: kfb, p to last st, kfb (2 sts inc).

Row 4: kfb, k to last st, kfb (2 sts inc).
Rep rows 3 and 4 three more times then row 3 once more (22 sts).
Beg with a k row, work 10 rows in st st.

Row 22: k2tog, k to last 2 sts, k2tog (2 sts dec).

Row 23: p2tog, p to last 2 sts, p2tog (2 sts dec).
Rep rows 22 and 23 until 4 sts rem.
Cast off.

Fin

Using 4mm (UK 8; US 6) and two strands of yarn A, cast on 2 sts.

Row 1 (WS): p to end.

Row 2 (RS): kfb, k to end (1 st inc).
Rep rows 1 and 2 nine more times (12 sts).

Row 21: k to end.

Row 22: k2tog, k to end (1 st dec).

Row 23: p to end.
Rep rows 22 and 23 until 2 sts rem.
Cast off.

To make up

1 With right sides together, stitch seam on ribbed section with a backstitch seam, then stitch side seams for approximately 7cm (2¾in), leaving the top open, for the mouth.

2 Turn right side out. Pin Mouth to open edges of both Jaws, then stitch in place.

3 Cut strips of felt to fit along the top and bottom edges of the Mouth and snip small triangular pieces from one long edge of each, for teeth.

4 Stitch the other long edge of the felt to the edges of the jaws.

5 Fold Fin in half along garter stitch ridge, with wrong sides together, and stitch edges together, then stitch the Fin to the Shark's back, using the photographs of the finished cover as a guide.

6 Fix eyes in place.

PIRATES

PIRATE COVER SET

These covers will appeal to the rebellious golfer, the nonconformist – or maybe the golfer whose game is all at sea. The skull and crossed clubs motif is designed to fit the driver, and you can make the jaunty striped companion covers in your own choice of colours.

Measurements and sizes

As for the basic cover on page 16. The instructions given are for a cover with a skull and crossed golf clubs motif to fit a driver, and a set of two striped covers to fit a 5-wood and a 3-wood.

YOU WILL NEED

- 100g of DK (light worsted/8-ply) yarn in black (A), 50g in white (B), blue (C), and red (D). Choose a double knitting yarn that knits to a standard DK (light worsted/8-ply) tension.
- Needles: 3.25mm (UK 10; US 3) and 4mm (UK 8; US 6)

TENSION

20 sts and 26 rows to 10cm (4in), measured over stocking stitch using 4mm (UK 8; US 6) needles, with two strands of yarn.

KNITTING THE COVERS

Driver

For the largest size (driver), using yarn A, follow the pattern for the basic cover, incorporating the intarsia motif in the straight, 21-row section in the centre part of the Head.

5-wood and 3-wood

For the other sizes, cast on using yarn A and follow the pattern for the ribbed section of the basic cover on page 18; change to 4mm (UK 8; US 6) needles and, using two strands of yarn, knit the Head in two-row stripes of yarns C and B, or C and D, using the photograph of the finished covers as a guide.

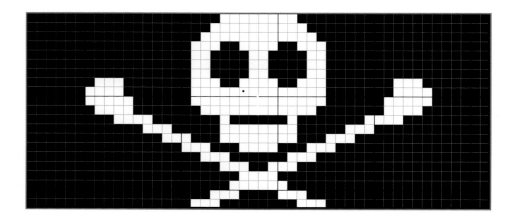

To make up

1 Pull up tail of yarn to gather stitches at top of cover. Fold cover in half with right sides together and stitch side edges together with a backstitch seam (alternatively, stitch seam from right side using mattress stitch). Turn right side out.

2 Weave in all yarn ends.

3 Add two nostrils to the skull on the driver cover with Swiss darning and yarn A.

Designed as a set, you can, of course, knit the striped covers on their own for less piratical purposes.

OCTOPUS COVER SET

The catch of the day – this subtly-coloured set of covers would also work well in the colours of your golf club.

Measurements and sizes

Separate instructions are given for covers to fit a 5-wood, a 3-wood and a driver.

TENSION

20 sts and 26 rows to 10cm (4in), measured over stocking stitch using 4mm (UK 8; US 6) needles and aran (worsted/10-ply) yarn.

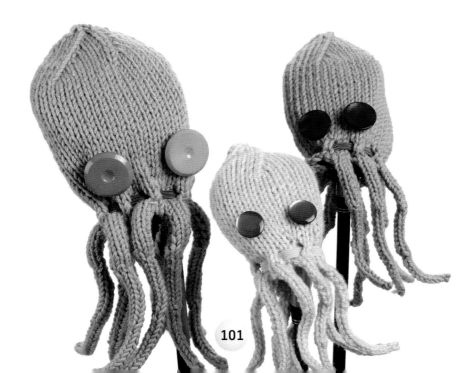

KNITTING THE COVERS

Tentacles

The tentacles are made using the i-cord method (see page 15)

Driver

Tentacles

Using two double-pointed 4mm (UK 8; US 6) needles and yarn A, cast on 3 sts.

Row 1: k3; do not turn but slide sts to other end of needle.

Rep row 1 eleven times more.

Row 13: k1, kfb, k1 (4 sts).

Work a further eleven rows using the i-cord method; turn.

Row 25: p to end.

Row 26: k2, M1, k2 (5 sts).

Beg with a p row, work eleven rows in st st.

Cut yarn and leave sts on a holder.

Make seven more Tentacles; do not cut yarn after completing the last one.

Body

Row 1 (RS): k all sts on needle, then, with RS facing, knit across all sts on a holder (40 sts).

Row 2: (p8, p2tog) to end (36 sts).

Row 3 (eyelets): k1, (yo, k2tog) to last st, k1.

To complete, follow the basic pattern on page 18 for Head section.

Medium

Tentacles

Using two double-pointed 4mm (UK 8; US 6) needles and yarn B, cast on 2 sts.

Row 1: k2, do not turn but slide sts to other end of needle.

Rep row 1 nine times more.

Row 11: k1, kfb (3 sts).

Work a further nine rows using the i-cord method; turn.

Row 21: p to end.

Row 26: kfb, k2 (4 sts).

Beg with a p row, work eleven rows in st st; cut yarn and leave sts on a holder

Make seven more Tentacles; do not cut yarn after completing the last one.

Body

Row 1 (RS): k all sts on needle, then, with RS facing, knit across all sts on a holder (32 sts).

Row 2: (p14, p2tog) twice (30 sts).

Row 3 (eyelets): k1, (yo, k2tog) to last st, k1.

To complete, follow the basic pattern on page 18 for Head section.

Small

Tentacles

Using two double-pointed 4mm (UK 8; US 6) needles and yarn C, cast on 2 sts.

Row 1: k2, do not turn but slide sts to other end of needle.

Rep row 1 seven times more.

Row 9: k1, kfb (3 sts).

Work a further 7 rows using the i-cord method; turn.

Beg with a p row, work thirteen rows in st st; cut yarn and leave sts on a holder.

Make seven more Tentacles; do not cut yarn after completing the last one.

Body

Row 1 (RS): k all sts on needle, then, with RS facing, knit across all sts on holder (24 sts).

Row 2: p to end.

Row 3 (eyelets): k1, (yo, k2tog) to last st, k1.
To complete, follow the basic pattern (page 18) for Head section.

To make up

1 Pull up tail of yarn to gather stitches at top of cover, then fold cover in half with right sides together and stitch seam in backstitch.

2 Dealing with each of the yarn ends at the top of the Tentacles in turn, neaten the joins with a few stitches, then weave in all ends.

3 Attach the buttons as eyes.

GOLDEN BEAR

BEAR COVER

During the 1967 US Open, an Australian sportswriter labelled Jack Nicklaus 'Golden Bear' in reference to his blond hair. Nicklaus's high school mascot had been a golden bear, and he was happy to accept the new nickname. Make your own big bear cover in a honey-coloured yarn.

Measurements and sizes

The instructions given are for a cover to fit a driver.

YOU WILL NEED

- 100g of DK (light worsted/8-ply) yarn in honey (A), and small amount of DK (light worsted/8-ply) yarn in black (B). Choose a double knitting yarn that knits to a standard DK (light worsted/8-ply) tension.
- Needles: 3.25mm (UK 10; US 3) and 4mm (UK 8; US 6)
- Toy stuffing
- Two black toy safety eyes
- Tapestry needle

TENSION

20 sts and 26 rows to 10cm (4in), measured over stocking stitch using 4mm (UK 8; US 6) needles and two strands of DK (light worsted/8-ply) yarn.

KNITTING THE COVER

Follow the pattern for the basic cover on page 18, using one strand of yarn A for the ribbed section and two strands for the Head.

Muzzle

Using 4mm (UK 8; US 6) needles and two strands of yarn A, cast on 6 sts.

Row 1 and each odd-numbered row: p to end.

Row 2 (RS): (kfb) to end (12 sts).

Row 4: (kfb) to end (24 sts).

Row 6: (k3, kfb) to end (30 sts).

Row 8: (k4, kfb) to end (36 sts).

Row 10: (k5, kfb) to end (42 sts).

Row 12: (k6, kfb) to end (48 sts).
Beg with a p row, work 3 rows in st st.
Cast off.

Ear (make 4)

Using 3.25mm needles and yarn A, cast on 16 sts.

Row 1 (RS): k each st tbl.
Beg with a p row, work 11 rows in st st.

Row 13: k1, skpo, k to last 3 sts, k2tog, k1 (2 sts dec).

Row 14: p to end.
Rep rows 13 and 14 three more times (8 sts).

Cast off.

Nose

Using 3.25mm (UK 10; US 3) needles and one strand of yarn B, cast on 2 sts.

Row 1: (kfb) twice (4 sts).

Row 2: k to end.

Row 3: kfb, k to last st, kfb (2 sts inc).
Rep rows 2 and 3 three more times (12 sts).

Row 10: k to end.
Cast off.

To make up

1 Pull up tail of yarn to gather stitches at top of cover. Fold cover in half with right sides together and stitch side edges together with a backstitch seam (alternatively, stitch seam from right side using mattress stitch). Turn right side out.

2 Stitch Muzzle in place, adding stuffing as you go. Gather cast-off edge of Nose slightly and stitch Nose in place, adding a tiny bit of stuffing to pad out shape.

3 Embroider a mouth in chain stitch, using yarn B and referring to the photograph of the finished cover.

4 Insert safety eyes just above the top edge of the Muzzle, and use washers to lock securely in place on the reverse.

5 Place two Ears right sides together and stitch together round curved edge, leaving cast-on edge unstitched. Turn right sides out and stitch straight edge to side of head.

*Details of the
muzzle, nose and mouth.*

GOLF BALL HOLDERS

GOLF BALL HOLDERS

While you have your needles and yarn at the ready, here is a pattern for a handy pouch for storing golf balls. The instructions here – which require you to knit in the round using four double-pointed needles – are given for a 4-ball and a 6-ball holder, but you can make your ball holder any length you like; just add another seventeen rounds for each additional ball.

Measurements and sizes

The instructions given are for a cover to fit a 4-ball holder, with instructions for the larger 6-ball holder given in brackets.

The 4-ball holder measures 22cm (8¾in) in length; the 6-ball holder measures 33cm (13in) in length.

TENSION

24 sts and 30 rows to 10cm (4in), measured over stocking stitch using 3.25mm (UK 10; US 3) needles, with a single strand of yarn.

KNITTING THE HOLDERS

Using 3.25mm (UK 10; US 3) doubl-pointed needles, cast on 24 sts and distribute between three of the needles (8 sts per needle), using the fourth to knit with.

Rounds 1 and 2: k to end.

Round 3 (eyelets): (yfwd, k2tog) to end. Knit 68 (102) rounds.

Next round (eyelets): (yfwd, k2tog) to end. Knit 1 round.

Cast off.

To make up

1 Weave in yarn ends.

2 Cut elastic into two equal lengths, thread one piece through eyelets at each end of the pouch, and stitch ends of elastic together.

3 Attach the clasp to the pouch.

4-ball holder.

6-ball holder.

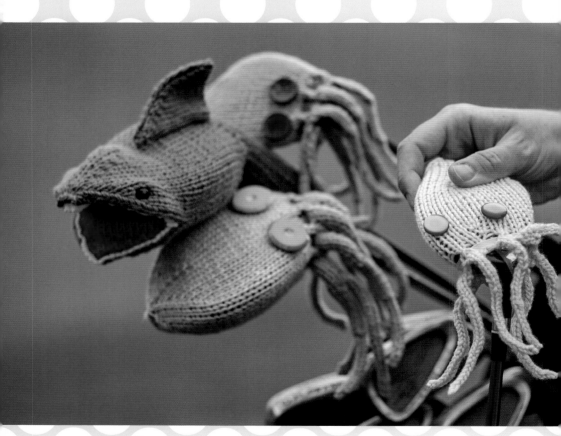

Sets of covers

Whether you're knitting a cover for yourself or as a gift, it's worth thinking about how it will be used. While a single cover is great for protecting your prized club, a set can make it quicker to identify and select clubs as you play – or just act as a way to personalise your bag. The examples on this page show just a few examples of themed sets made using the covers in this book.

First published in Great Britain 2018

Search Press Limited
Wellwood, North Farm Road,
Tunbridge Wells, Kent TN2 3DR

Text copyright © Susie Johns 2018

Photographs by Roddy Paine Photographic Studios.
Search Press would like to thank Dale Hill Hotel and
Golf Club, Ticehurst, UK, for use of their grounds.

Photographs and design copyright
© Search Press Ltd. 2018

ISBN: 978-1-78221-494-6

Publisher's Note
The Publishers and author can accept no responsibility for
any consequences arising from the information, advice or
instructions given in this publication.

Readers are permitted to reproduce any of the items in this
book for their personal use, or for the purposes of selling for
charity, free of charge and without the prior permission of the
Publishers. Any use of the items for commercial purposes is not
permitted without the prior permission of the Publishers.

Suppliers
If you have difficulty in obtaining any of the materials and
equipment mentioned in this book, then please visit the
Search Press website for details of suppliers:
www.searchpress.com

Printed in China through Asia Pacific Offset

Dedication

*To Steve Paxman, Jason Macey and
Professor Bob Gilchrist, in appreciation of
their valuable advice and insight into the
mysterious world of golf and golfers.*

Acknowledgements

*Thanks to Rico yarns for supplying Rico Essentials
Merino DK yarns, to King Cole for supplying
Merino Blend DK, and to Designer Yarns for
supplying Debbie Bliss Rialto DK.*